Notes In My Back Pocket

Jackie Goneze

BookLeaf Publishing

Presentation by *BookLeaf Publishing*

Web: www.bookleafpub.com

E-mail: info@bookleafpub.com

ISBN: 9789357215107

First edition 2022

Dedicated to all the worthy babes who have felt less than from wearing their hearts on their sleeves. You're worth it.

ACKNOWLEDGEMENT

To my loved ones who guided me in the past, to my loved ones who guide me in the now, to my loved ones who will guide me in the future…

I love you deeply.

PREFACE

“Earn your own respect. It takes ages, it’s a constant and worthy battle and it’s by far the hardest to win.”

— Joanna Cannon, Three Things I’d Tell My Younger Self

Bisou

I googled how to French kiss.

Just for you.

You didn't know how to either.

The warm September breeze nudged me to you.

We laughed.

Walked another block… to delay the loss of
simple innocence.

My pink shirt.

Your backpack hanging low.

The shrubs where that empty lot use to be,

Blurred my peripheral.

I giggled.

You smiled.

We agreed to practice together.

We agreed we had all the time in the world.

Even if it wasn’t that day.

We could have any day beyond that.

You leaned in.

I closed my eyes.

You kissed me softly.

That was still new, your kisses.

Butterflies.

You parted my lips with yours.

&

We French kissed.

Entry

You couldn't even be my friend,

Yet... I allowed you to be more.

That's when it ended,

You became a brick wall with no door.

Lying to myself

"I have no expectations," I lied.

I

had

already

imagined

years down the line.

Faceless

they never had a face
the future lovers we would conjure up
for ourselves
in the late nights
or early mornings
conversation that never went further
past where we are now in life
we would have been tucked away
in our blankets
the warmth of the blue
hue in any tiny room
where we spoke
that felt endless in holding all our secret desires
that we did not yet have an idea about
we knew no one would ever be completely
perfect so we chose their flaws
where we could manage
and if we needed to hurt
we could still grow
and they would love use deeply
endlessly though faceless
we knew we wanted love
and warmth
and growth
and something special

Mwen pa ase?

What did I do to deserve this?

Was I too faithful? Too kind? Just cute? And not fine?

Care too much? Love too hard? Smother and push you far?

Why did I not deserve to be loved by you everyday until there were no more left?

I poured into you and I loved you and dug into my deepest depths.

I wasn't worthy.

I wasn't enough.
I wasn't enough.
I wasn't enough, for you.

Everywhere

How are you everywhere like this?

I don’t even search for you.

Your face in every crowded crevice.

My mind not sure on what to do.

Loss

Rupi wrote, “if I’m not the love of your life I’ll
be the greatest loss instead”
With that said, I had wished you sleepless nights
filled with tossing and turning and tear soaked
pillows
I had wished you nightmares, if sleep did greet
you, of what should have been that you no
longer deserved
I had wished you nausea and shortness of breath,
sweaty palms and mind full of regret
I had wished you bloody knees from groveling
to come back to me.
And I’d be here with a mirage of open arms and
I would have the greatest strength of moving on
I had wished you greatness too but one that
would never equate to mine. Because I’d prove
to be better without you and wished that your
successes weren’t fulfilling without me. It would
feel like a crime.
I wished that you’d realize that you needed me
and wanted me and loved me the way I did you.

Duck duck goose

/You/ chose her over me.
-You- did too.
And maybe *you*?
But now there's no way to ever know the truth.

Skeptical

The first time

I “broke” your heart,

how did you heal?

Uncomfortable

you held me against the fence

kissed me

and

instead of butterflies I felt nauseas

Feeling blindsided I stormed off angrily

She didn't deserve that

Neither did I

Unsafe and unsure of your motives

I started avoiding you

Coming up with excuses

Coming up with lies

I didn't trust your boundaries

I didn't think they existed

You scared me

And that felt unnatural for us

Love for me

I wish I could mold

all the hurt,

lingering love,

worry and care into a gift of love for myself.

Not just a piece like I did do.

The entire bulk of it.

So much so,

that there isn't space

for you in me at all.

Supposed to be

You were supposed to be my best friend
Have my back
Get on my nerves
Tell me when I'm wrong
Allow me to do the same
Love me in a way that was free of pain
That best friend shit
Be Uncle
Me, be aunty
Family... carved from years
Our moms would've gotten along
A little too much for our liking
But nah
You wanted more
And left me behind
And now I'm tight
I lost you in the way we should've had each other
I listened to you when I was right
I was always right
I was always looking out for you
And you only looked out for you
It's obvious that I'm stuck
On a person I became disposable to
I wish you were disposable to me too

You were supposed to be my best friend
But you replaced me with an enabler
Someone who you couldn't even learn to grow
from
That's life I guess.

Love bombed

"If you leave me, I'll kill myself..."

Carefree

The part of my heart that misses you isn't just remembering the past.

It wants to be young.

And playful.

And curious.

And carefree.

And with you, I was all of that.

What ifs

What ifs...
How many times can your heart be wrenched to where it implodes in you?
How many times can you be deceived that everything is okay when it isn't?
You want it to be okay, you pray it'll be okay but for some reason when all isn't said and you go pretending and go with the "motions" of everything that is supposedly usual it sadly doesn't make it okay.
I don't know how much more fight I have left in me to hold back the tears I've been holding for a week now.
Yeah a week.
When you really love someone that enough is a burden on the heart.
It takes over your mind, your heart, your body, your everything.
And Love is never only that feeling of happiness.
Every other emotion and feeling is there.
And with him it's only been a whirlpool of emotions and what hurts the most is that loving him is a taboo.

We both think of, dream of our what ifs... but that's all they will ever be.
What ifs.
I don't want that.
I want my what ifs to happen but without risking everything else.
Unfortunately just having feelings bought risk to us and our friendship.
Last night we came to our final temporary goodbyes.
I say temporary cause I can't see him out of my life... He said I'll try not to be a complete stranger...among novels of other things he wrote.
I couldn't even open my mouth without risking a sob in a room full of people.
Why did we fall knowing we wouldn't be able to be caught?
Landing hurt so much and its in getting up you see how strong you are.
I can't get up.
I've lost my best friend and I am hurt.
Sad.
Lonely.
Angry.
Scared.
And I can't stop thinking about What ifs....

Closure

c l o s u r e does not exist.
c l o s u r e does not exist.
c l o s u r e does not exist.
c l o s u r e does not exist.
c l o s u r e does not exist.

stop expecting that the answers to your questions
will satisfy you.

Keywords part one

Youth
Round one & two
Justin Nozuka - After Tonight
Yellow Fanta
B17
Winter stories
Jolly ranchers
Play fighting
Michael Jackson - PYT
Rebound
Macy's
Rihanna feat Future - Loveeeeeee song

Keywords part two

High School
Round one & two
Tamia feat Fabolous - So into you
Tattoo
Love notes
Moonlight
Notebooks
White Chocolate
Experience
Mural
A 'last time'

To you

I want to believe that the past present and future
all happen simultaneously.

So when I look back and appreciate you better,
I hope that you feel it.
And maybe it will change
how I see myself now.
I want you to know,
you who is me at
13, 14, 15, 16, 17, 18, 19, 20, 21…
that it turns out okay.
That you are worthy of all the things love bring.
All the things friendship brings.
All the things that loyalty brings.
You are worthy of it.

Now I will wait for you to believe it then… so
that I can believe it now.

I care too much

I care too much.
I’m too honest.
I’m too caring.
I’m too loving.
I’m too involved.
I’m too much of things that I shouldn’t be.
I’m too far from where I need to be.
I’m too sad.
I’m too deep in pain.
I’m over everything.

21

at 21
i told myself
that third times the charm
& i got that chance with you

to the sun ☀️ the stars ✨ the moon 🌙 &
beyond ❤️

www.ingramcontent.com/pod-product-compliance
Lightning Source LLC
Chambersburg PA
CBHW051752130826
49812CB00033B/1117
* 9 7 8 9 3 5 7 2 1 5 1 0 7 *